On the Farm

Edited by Gillian Doherty
With thanks to Rupert Aker from the Soil Association
for information about farming.

On the Farm

Anna Milbourne

Illustrated by Alessandra Roberti

Designed by Laura Parker

Can you imagine what it's like
to live on a farm?

As the sun comes up, the rooster crows...

cock-a-doodle-doo

...and everyone in the
farmhouse begins to stir.

The cows come plodding
slowly down the lane.

Their warm breath
steams in the morning air.

Mooing and stomping their heavy feet,
the cows line up in the milking barn.

The farmer puts tubes
onto their pink udders...

...and their creamy milk
 is sucked into a cool tank.

A big tanker-truck rumbles into the farmyard.

The driver pumps the fresh milk
into the tanker and takes it away to be sold.

Next, it's time to feed the hens.

They peck-peck-peck
at the scattered corn.

Inside the little henhouse, nestled in the straw...

...are three warm, speckled eggs.

There are some new baby lambs over in the barn.
Two are sucking milk from their mother...

...and waggling their woolly tails happily.

But there's no room
for the littlest one...

...so she has to be fed from a baby's bottle.
Soon, her tail starts waggling too.

Outside, the sheepdog is guiding
the sheep to a sunny meadow.

The farmer whistles
to tell him which way to run.

The dog crouches quietly at the gate
as the sheep trot through...

...and start to munch
on the long, green grass.

The tractor is chugging up and down in the next field.

It's planting lots of seeds in rows.

Hungry little birds
would like to eat the seeds...

...but the scarecrow
scares them all away.

Some plants are already growing
under a big, warm shelter.

There are tomato plants
(but no tomatoes yet)...

...and bean plants
with pretty flowers
(but not a single bean).

But there's plenty of lettuce
that's ready to eat.

The children pick
the biggest one
to take home.

As the sun sinks down behind the hills...

...the hens cluck sleepily
and go inside their henhouse.

The tractor comes chugging
across the field...

...and the farmer and his sheepdog
trudge back home.

Everyone kicks off their muddy boots and scrambles inside. It's been a very busy day.

Would you like to live on a farm?